PAIN OF A PARTICULAR KIND

PAIN OF A PARTICULAR KIND

THE LOSS OF A CHILD

Peter Barnes

THE BANNER OF TRUTH TRUST

THE BANNER OF TRUTH TRUST

Head Office
3 Murrayfield Road
Edinburgh, EH12 6EL
UK

North America Office
610 Alexander Spring Road
Carlisle, PA 17015
USA

banneroftruth.org

First published 2024

*

ISBN
Print: 978 1 80040 456 4
Epub: 978 1 80040 457 1

*

Typeset in 12/15 Minion Pro
at The Banner of Truth Trust, Edinburgh

Printed in the USA by
Versa Press Inc.,
East Peoria, IL.

For

EMILY ELIZABETH SO

(29 November 2016 – 24 May 2022)

in the hands of the Good Shepherd

Contents

Introduction: How This Book Came to Be Written

I am married to Lyn, and we have six grown-up children (Matthew, Graham, Luke, Heather, Paul, and Clare, and eleven grandchildren on earth). A grievous blow struck our family on 24 May 2022 when five-year-old Emily So (a much-loved daughter of BJ and Heather So) died of a terminal brain tumour (DIPG) after a seven-month struggle with the disease. On 24 May 1738 John Wesley felt his heart 'strangely warmed'; on 24 May 2022 the So and Barnes families felt their hearts desperately grieved.

This little work has had three lives, as it were. It began as an article which was written soon after our fifth child, Paul, had open-heart surgery on 24 December 1986, the day after he was born. Against medical probability, this mercifully saved his life, although there were months of anxiety which followed. The issue of infant salvation was naturally much in my mind.[1] Nearly thirty years later, in 2013, in order to meet other needs, the article was updated and expanded, and self-published.[2] But after the deeply felt loss of dear Emily, it has been revised again, and reworked with a peculiar and personal pain added.

To that extent, it has been an almost excruciating work to write – to immerse oneself in floods of pain, to revisit the sense of helplessness, to fight to maintain a joyous belief in a sovereign and good God. Always inadequate, as we all are, I have never felt so inadequate. C. S. Lewis once commented that 'apologetic work is so dangerous to one's own faith. A doctrine never seems dimmer to me than when I have just successfully defended it.'[3] This is not a work of apologetics, but a brief attempt to understand and work through grief, for myself, my family, and for any other readers. It has only heightened the sense of my own need to receive comfort myself. Such comfort can only come from the God who is our creator and our redeemer.

[1] Peter Barnes, 'The Loss of a Child' in *The Banner of Truth*, Issue 292, January 1988, pp. 16-22.

[2] Peter Barnes, *The Loss of a Child* (Sydney, 2013).

[3] C. S. Lewis, *Letters*, ed. by W. H. Lewis (San Diego: Harcourt Brace Jovanovich, 1966), p. 209.

The hope remains that God will use this book to minister to and bless any of his people who have suffered the agony of losing a child.

Preface

Life is not what we want it to be. Even in what we call 'good times', there is more than a sneaking suspicion that pain and trouble are lurking nearby. Joni Eareckson Tada, who has been a quadriplegic since breaking her neck after diving into shallow water in 1967, has looked at life, and commented: 'It's a fragile house of cards, and we keep praying that nobody bumps the table.'[1] Sometimes what we fear most is precisely what happens. It may be that someone 'bumps the table', as it were, but ultimately that someone is God himself. He kills and he makes alive, but he works all things for good (cf. Deut. 32:39; Isa. 45:7; Gen. 50:20; note Mark 7:37). How do we go about picking up the cards and rebuilding the house? Nothing is the same; our fragility now has neon lights. We are afraid. It is as Vaneetha Rendall Risner said: 'Grieving may

[1] Joni Eareckson Tada, with Larry Libby, *A Spectacle of Glory* (Michigan: Zondervan, 2016), October 23, p. 320.

be the most difficult work you'll do on earth.'[2] How does one find grace and joy in a fog, or worse, in a nightmare?

There are few things which any parent dreads more than the thought of outliving his or her child, or grandchild. The deaths of parents, friends, relatives and even one's spouse are terrible indeed, but the death of one's child possesses a peculiar kind of horror. In Dostoevsky's *The Brothers Karamazov*, the unbelieving Ivan challenges Alyosha at just this point. It is the suffering of helpless children that Ivan refers to as the awful argument against the providence of the God of the Bible who is both good and just.[3] It is an unsettling claim, and deserves more than a glib answer.

The great men of faith are not immune to this kind of suffering – Thomas Boston outlived six of his ten children, and John Owen outlived all eleven of his. Charles Spurgeon's mother actually gave birth to seventeen children, but nine died in infancy. Indeed, even in this age of advanced technology in much of the Western world, it is by

[2] Vaneetha Rendall Risner, 'To Anyone Who Has lost a Child', 14 July 2020, desiringGod.

[3] Fyodor Dostoevsky, *The Brothers Karamazov*, trans. by David McDuff (London: Penguin, 2003), Book V, chap. 4, e.g. pp. 316-21.

no means uncommon for children to die before their parents. Always, the comfort for the Christian is that expressed by B. M. Palmer, the renowned Southern Presbyterian preacher in nineteenth-century America, who lost an infant son and four of his five daughters. On the death of one of his daughters, he declared: 'We think of her not as dead, but as translated to be with Christ.'[4] This is the Christian hope, without which life is ultimately a meaningless tragedy.

[4] B. M. Palmer, *The Broken Home: Lessons in Sorrow* (1890; repr. Harrisonburg, VA: Sprinkle, 1981), p. 48.

1

The Sorrow of Losing a Child

Suffering and death are part of this fallen sinful world. In fact, they are the evidence that this world, created very good by our Creator, is now infested with sin – and sin has its consequences. Preaching on 2 Timothy 1:7, John Chrysostom declared:

> For there is no such thing in this mortal life as being exempt from sorrow. If not today, yet tomorrow; if not tomorrow, yet some later day trouble comes. For as one cannot sail, I mean, over a long sea, and not feel disquietude, so it is not possible to pass through this life without experience of sorrow …[1]

We have been cast out of the Garden of Eden.

Death is our fiercest and last enemy; it is an all-consuming monster. We withdraw in horror

[1] John Chrysostom, *Homilies on Timothy*, Oxford edition with additions by Philip Schaff, in *Nicene and Post-Nicene Fathers*, vol. XIII (Grand Rapids, MI: Eerdmans, 1979), on 2 Timothy 1:7, p. 477 (slightly modernized).

at the thought of life ending, and of our being ushered into what Job called 'the land of darkness and the shadow of death' (Job 10:21). The American Presbyterian, R. A. Webb, spoke for all when he wrote:

> I hate death; I hate it everywhere – in garden, meadow, swamp, and human home; it violates every noble thing in me; it is a death's head which makes me shudder in every fibre of my being; it is a repulsive thing which makes me recoil in terror upon myself; it shadows all my ideas, and plunges me into companionship with worms that crawl and gnaw in the darkness of the grave; it is the one thing that tempts my frightened soul to cry out, 'God owes me an apology for giving me life, if I, and all things else, must die.' Why must any human being lie down and die?[2]

As Job put it: 'Why is light given to him who is in misery?' (Job 3:20).

Yet God has no pleasure in the death of anyone (Ezek. 18:32). The Lord Jesus, who is the resurrection and the life, wept at the tomb of Lazarus, so moved was he by tenderness and sympathy – and even a kind of anger – at the death of his disciple and friend (John 11:35). The Word became flesh and

[2] R. A. Webb, *The Theology of Infant Salvation* (1907; repr. Harrisonburg, VA: Sprinkle, 1981), p. 71.

tabernacled among us, and the apostles beheld his glory, the glory as the only Son from the Father, full of grace and truth – and he shed tears.

Nothing appals us more than death, and no death more so than the death of a child. We can become partly immunised to aged adults dying, but children are not meant to die. If there are few joys that can match the birth of a child, there are few sorrows that can match the death of a child. When the 'blood and iron' Chancellor of Germany in the late nineteenth century, Otto von Bismarck, was asked what gave him most satisfaction in life, he did not reply in terms of his political achievements, such as they were. Rather, he said, 'That God did not take away any of my children.'[3] It is not a Christian response, but it is one with which we can empathise.

No grief matches that of a parent who has lost a child. Dr C. Everett Koop was a man of deep Reformed convictions regarding the goodness and sovereignty of God, but in 1968 he lost his twenty-year-old son, David, in a rock climbing accident, and came to attest to the fact that 'there is nothing in the world that comes anywhere near the

[3] Cited in A. J. P. Taylor, *A Personal History* (London: Coronet Books, 1984), pp. 347-48.

experience of losing your own child.'[4] The house has a new and terrible quietness, and for a time life becomes an empty ordeal. In the picturesque description of the Psalmist, we feel 'like a wineskin in the smoke' (Psa. 119:83) – dried up and useless. Mealtimes can be particularly difficult, and special occasions may become almost unbearable.

A tragedy similar to that suffered by the Koop household struck Nicholas Wolterstorff and his family. Wolterstorff taught Philosophical Theology at Yale University, but his world was shattered when one of his five children, his twenty-five-year-old son, Eric, was killed in a mountain-climbing accident. Twelve years after the tragedy, Wolterstorff said the wound was no longer raw, but it remained as 'this endless neverness'[5] – an irreplaceable person is gone. Wolterstorff has a way with words, and he records that the family committed Eric into 'the tender resurrected resurrecting hands of Jesus.'[6]

Some further quotations from Wolterstorff's book are in order: 'All I can do is *remember* him. I can't *experience* him'; 'Sorrow is no longer the

[4] C. Everett and Elizabeth Koop, *Sometimes Mountains Move* (Milton Keynes: Word, 1979), p. 66.

[5] Nicholas Wolterstorff, *Lament for a Son* (Grand Rapids, MI: Eerdmans, 1987), p. 15.

[6] Ibid., p. 40.

islands but the sea' (p. 7); 'I've become an alien in the world, shyly touching it as if it's not mine. I don't belong any more. When someone loved leaves home, home becomes mere house' (p. 51); 'Wounded love is special love' (p. 59); 'I do not know why God would watch him fall' (p. 68); 'In commanding us to love, God invites us to suffer' (p. 89); and finally 'The tears of God are the meaning of history' (p. 90). Love and faith and suffering are all intertwined in the heart of Wolterstorff, and articulated in a way that few can emulate but all can ponder.

On 3 November 2020 Tim Challies and his family lost their son, Nick, to a sudden heart attack when he was an apparently fit young twenty-year-old. He was engaged to be married and he was studying at the Southern Baptist Theological Seminary in Louisville, Kentucky – and the Lord took him. Challies pondered John 12:24, 25, that the seed dies before it comes to life. Burying his son was deeply painful, but he wrote: 'The hope rising in my heart as I watch my son being sown into the earth is the hope of resurrection.'[7] 'Thy will be done,' is the prayer of the Christian, yet Nick's death left his

[7] Tim Challies, *Seasons of Sorrow* (Grand Rapids, MI: Zondervan, 2022), p. 21.

father saying: 'I fear God and I am afraid of God.'[8] Everyone we love – whether infant or aged – is a breath away from being taken by God who is both good and sovereign. Faith is rest in Christ (Matt. 11:28-30), but at times it can seem like rest on a roller coaster (note Job, Habakkuk, Psalm 73).

Life is a vale of tears. Recriminations and fault-finding may not be far away. In 2003 Barbara Ireland lost her three-year-old daughter, Laura, when she was left briefly in the family car while Barbara went into the family house in regional South Australia in order to collect a few things. Inexplicably, the car caught fire, and Laura perished.[9] 'Why did I leave her there?' and 'How could this happen to me?' The grieving parent knows the import of C. S. Lewis' graphic description of how he felt after the death of his wife: 'Her absence is like the sky, spread over everything.'[10] The family dynamics are changed; everything has shifted; the world has tilted on its axis.

We can only know what God reveals to us in his word; the secret things belong to him (Deut.

[8] Ibid., pp. 42-45.

[9] Barbara Ireland, *Daddy will carry me* (Sydney: Ark House Press, 2023).

[10] C. S. Lewis, *A Grief Observed* (London: Faber and Faber, 1966), p. 12.

29:29). The curtain is drawn aside a little in John 11 where Jesus eventually raises Lazarus from the tomb. Jesus loved Lazarus who was seriously ill (John 11:3, 5), yet the Lord seemed in no hurry to heal him. He delayed and by the time he arrived at Bethany, Lazarus had been dead four days (John 11:6, 39). Why the delay? Lazarus' two sisters came close to chiding the Saviour for his slow response (John 11:21, 32). Strange love! Yet Jesus says that it was for the good of his disciples (John 11:15, 41, 42). A demonstration of his resurrection power would prove of greater spiritual help than a healing (John 11:25, 26, 43, 44).

Was this why dear Emily was not healed? Was it to make all who knew her and loved her look for something greater? The 'why' question is beyond us, but we can answer 'For what purpose?' In 1986 our prayers for our newborn Paul were answered as we so ardently desired. In 2022 our prayers for young Emily were not answered as we desired with an equal ardour. Why? Why the terrible difference? We do not know. For what purpose? We can do better here. We are to testify to the hope that we have in Christ – that is true whether the child is spared or taken.

It remains a struggle – if we have faith the size of a mustard seed, Jesus tells us that mountains will be moved and we will receive what we ask for (Matt. 17:20, 21; 21:21, 22). Yet we also read that chastening is a sign that we are God's children (Heb. 12:7-11). The disciples tried to guess why the man born blind was born that way – was it because of his sin (in the womb!) or the sin of his parents – but Jesus takes them from past analysis to present living. This was so the works of God would be displayed in him (John 9:1-3). The one who trusts in Christ has the assurance that God is able to do far more abundantly than all that we ask or think (Eph. 3:20). We pray for healing, but he gives glory. Is that the answer? Is that your answer?

On 21 May 2008 – 'the day the world went wrong' – Mary Beth Chapman was busy working on the wedding plans for her eldest child, Emily. Her son, Will, pulled into the driveway and accidentally ran over his little sister, Maria, and killed her. The grief was almost unimaginably deep. There have been many times since then when Mary Beth has viewed life almost in terms of *Mary Beth versus God*. If God wanted to declare war on her life, she at least would rail back. Her husband, the Christian singer-songwriter, Steve Curtis Chapman, found some consolation in his music, and produced a haunting and powerful CD entitled *Beauty Will*

Rise where one song proclaims: 'Heaven is the face of a little girl' – somewhat like Boethius, who, facing execution in 524, wrote that he was 'driven by grief to shelter in sad songs.'[11] Similarly, but with a more hostile anguish, Mary Beth identified with the struggles of the Psalmist and with Job, before finally agonising her way to 'Taste and see that the Lord is good' (Psa. 34:8).[12] But the first response could not be Psalm 34:8 or Romans 8:28. It had to be a night of weeping and questioning before the dawn would break.

In many people, this sense of desolation and loss can be overwhelming. The Bible tells of how Joseph was sold into slavery by his brothers who then lied to their father, Jacob, telling him that Joseph had been killed by a wild animal. So great was Jacob's grief that he refused to be comforted, and declared that he would go down to his grave mourning (Gen. 37:35). Such unrelieved sorrow is, alas, not peculiar to Jacob. When G. K. Chesterton's sister, Beatrice, died at the age of eight, Chesterton's father responded by turning Beatrice's picture to the wall, getting rid of all her

[11] Boethius, *The Consolation of Philosophy*, trans. by V. E. Watts (Harmondsworth: Penguin, 1978), Book 1, p. 35.

[12] See Mary Beth Chapman with Ellen Vaughn, *Choosing to SEE* (Grand Rapids: Revell, 2010), especially, pp. 12, 21, 146.

possessions, and forbidding anyone to mention her name.[13]

Nor is the torment any the less when the dead child is much younger. Dostoevsky's daughter, Sonya, was only three months old when she died, but three days after her burial, the great Russian novelist wrote these tender words:

> This little three-month-old creature, so poor, so tiny, was already a person and a character for me. She was beginning to know me, to love, and smile when I came near. When with my comical voice I used to sing songs to her, she liked to listen to them ... But where is Sonya? Where is this little personality for whom, I say boldly, I would accept the cross's agony if only she might be alive.[14]

The Virgin Mary herself was told that a sword would pierce through her own soul, meaning that she would suffer in living to see the death of her Son (Luke 2:35).

Grief is an awful burden to bear, but it is a part of our fallen world, and we must expect it. When Job lost his ten children, his grief was very

[13] A. S. Dale, *The Outline of Sanity: A Life of G. K. Chesterton* (Michigan: Eerdmans, 1982), p. 7.

[14] K. Mochulsky, *Dostoevsky: His Life and Work*, trans. by M. A. Minihan (New Jersey: Princeton University Press), 1973), pp. 332-33.

great (Job 1:20; 2:13), as was that of the widow of Nain who lost her only son (Luke 7:13). The Bible everywhere assumes that the person who has lost a dear one will grieve, and nowhere criticises such grief. Yet, for the Christian, grief and sorrow must not give way to despair. The apostle Paul distinguishes between the sorrow of those who have no hope and that of Christians who have a sure and certain hope (1 Thess. 4:13). Many tombs in the ancient world bear the inscription: 'I was not and I was, I am not and I care not.'[15] Unbelief takes refuge in bravado or sentimentality; Christianity faces reality with compassion.

When his wife Sarah died, Abraham, the father of faith, mourned and wept for her (Gen. 23:2). David's grief over the death of his son Absalom was so intense that he could not carry out his public duties as king until Joab rebuked him (2 Sam. 18:33–19:1-8). There is a warning in Leviticus 19:28 where God forbids his people to cut their bodies for the dead. Derek Tidball thinks that this refers only to the worship of ancestors,[16] but Gordon Wenham is correct in connecting it also to pagan mourning

[15] Cited in Jeffrey A. D. Weima, 1–2 Thessalonians (Grand Rapids, MI: Baker, 2014), p. 315.

[16] Derek Tidball, *The Message of Leviticus* (Leicester: IVP, 2005), p. 246.

rites.[17] In 1674 John Flavel, who himself lost a child, and who wrote a book for a woman who had lost her only child, spent much of his treatise distinguishing between a godly moderate sorrow and an ungodly immoderate sorrow.[18] These adjectives do not seem to be the most suitable ones to use. A moderate sorrow might imply a moderate love, which is not what the Bible commends. Certainly, we must weep but not wail, although the distinction is sometimes clearer in Flavel's work than in the believer's experience – something which Flavel himself recognised.

For the Christian, there is indeed sorrow – the most intense sorrow – but there is also hope. Underneath are the everlasting arms, and these arms set a definite limit to grief. God is compassionate and all-powerful, and he has determined our length of days here on earth before there was ever one of them (Psa. 139:16). In him there is safety, eternal safety. As the hymn puts it in speaking of departed saints:

[17] Gordon J. Wenham, *The Book of Leviticus* (Grand Rapids, MI: Eerdmans, 1979), p. 272.

[18] John Flavel, *Facing Grief* (Edinburgh: Banner of Truth Trust, 2010). Flavel's work was originally published as *A Token for Mourners*. It is interesting how often he cites the Stoic philosopher, Seneca.

We feebly struggle, they in glory shine.[19]

With an eye for just the right text, Flavel pointed mourners to Luke 7:13, 'And when the Lord saw her, he had compassion on her, and said unto her, Weep not.' There is the distress of a sorrowing woman, the compassion of our Saviour, and the power of his word soon to be demonstrated. The parent-child connection is so powerful that Flavel described children as 'the parent multiplied.'[20] Such a connection deepens the affliction, but the believer is assured as to how much deeper is the compassion and power of Christ (see Isa. 49:15).

In her own most empathetic way, Joni Eareckson Tada tells of the mystery, the vulnerability, and the glorious power of the Christian faith. When she was only five years of age – Emily's age – Joni's niece, Kelly, was struck down with brain cancer – Emily's disease. In February 1970 the little girl died, at the very time when Joni was still pondering her own diving accident of 1967, which had left her in hospital for two years and a quadriplegic for life.[21] How is a Christian to understand this? Not just

[19] From 'For All the Saints' by William Walsham How (1823–97).

[20] Flavel, *Facing Grief*, p. 3.

[21] Joni Eareckson Tada, *Joni* (Sydney: Strand Publishing, 2001), pp. 130-31.

what would be viewed as an untimely death, but death at a time when the Eareckson family was already reeling from the hammer blow of sudden and terrible suffering. Joni, of course, never forgot the passing of her young niece, and later recorded that on the night she died, at two o'clock in the morning, 'I saw a brilliant, golden shape flash pass the window.'[22] Angels are ministering spirits sent out to serve those who will inherit salvation (Heb. 1:14). Joni raises the possibility that this was one of those rare occasions when the angel was seen, at least in the form of a brilliant flash. The God who afflicts is the God who also greatly comforts.

[22] Joni Eareckson Tada, *The God I Love* (Grand Rapids: Zondervan, 2003), p. 206.

2

God's Answers to Our Questions

In response to suffering, many people try to say that all adversity comes from the devil – or at least that it does not come from God. The influential William Barclay declared that 'pain and suffering are never the will of God for his children.'[1] In fact, he considered the very idea to be blasphemous. It is true that God does not afflict his people willingly (literally, 'from the heart'); he does not delight to send trouble and sorrow (Lam. 3:33). However, he is utterly sovereign, and we must face the fact that even in the death of a child, the Lord is working out his eternal purposes for good. Barclay's view cuts God off from the world, and renders him, in Augustine's vivid expression, 'cruelly weak.'[2] The

[1] William Barclay, *Testament of Faith* (Oxford: Mowbray, 1977), pp. 44-45.

[2] Cited in Peter Brown, *Augustine of Hippo*, revised edition (London: Faber and Faber, 2000), p. 397.

Bible's teaching is that it is the Lord who forms the light and creates the darkness, who makes peace and creates calamity; he does all these things (Isa 45:7). Woe and well-being both come from him (Lam. 3:38). Not even a sparrow falls to the ground apart from our Father's will (Matt. 10:29).

God whose nature is love (1 John 4:16) is also the one who does according to his will in the army of heaven and among the inhabitants of the earth (Dan. 4:35). What appears to be a problem – how can God be both good and sovereign? – is actually the solution – he is indeed both good and sovereign. The sorrowing Christian, amidst all his distress, is enabled to cling to a precious truth:

> Here in the maddening maze of things,
> When tossed by storm and flood,
> To one fixed ground my spirit clings;
> I know that God is good![3]

God is not cut off from the sorrow and suffering of his people. Far from it, Isaiah tells us that 'in all their affliction he was afflicted' (Isa. 63:9). The grieving parent hears Christ say: 'I was dead' (Rev. 1:18). The eternal Son of God has experienced what your child has experienced. There is a fellowship

[3] John Greenleaf Whittier (1807–92), from his poem 'The Eternal Goodness' (1867).

of sufferings (Phil. 3:10), as Christ's sufferings, as it were, are filled up by his people's afflictions (Col. 1:24). This vain, short and uncertain world will not have the last say. There is a Saviour who is alive for evermore (Rev. 1:18).

By the graveside of our little child, we might be tempted to ask: 'What good can God be achieving through this?' For the Christian, the answer is that 'all things work together for good to those who love God, to those who are the called according to his purpose' (Rom. 8:28). Death is not the worst calamity. When Abijah, the son of the wicked king Jeroboam, died, this took place precisely because the child was the only one in Jeroboam's household to find favour in God's sight (1 Kings 14:1, 12, 13).[4] This passage alone is enough to refute the notion that the death of the infant is evidence that he or she is not of the elect. John MacArthur tells of a sad and bizarre example of one ill-informed 'Calvinist'

[4] Gregory of Nyssa does not refer to this passage, but he does argue that by taking the life of an infant, God may be preserving that child from the foreseen evils of life, including the child's own indwelling sin (cf. Gregory of Nyssa, *On Infants' Early Deaths* in *Select Writings and Letters of Gregory, Bishop of Nyssa*, translated by William Moore and Henry Austin Wilson, in *Nicene and Post-Nicene Fathers*, second series, vol. V, [Grand Rapids, MI: Eerdmans, 1983], pp. 372-81).

who thought that his infant's death demonstrated that the child was not to be numbered among the elect.[5] Rather, the lesson is that God brings good out of evil, even out of death. All Christians know this, but it is rarely something that can be immediately or easily embraced in the face of death. Those who apply the balm of Romans 8:28 in a facile way lose something of their humanity.

The Bible assures us that suffering in the Christian produces perseverance, character, and hope which does not disappoint (Rom. 5:3-5). If you have lost a child, you will be wounded for the rest of your earthly life, but that is not the end of the story. Jacob wrestled all night with a man who was God – surely a pre-incarnation appearance of the Son of God in the Old Testament (Gen. 32:22-32). The result was that Jacob walked with a limp for the rest of his life, yet he was blessed by God. Somehow, God works his blessing by means of suffering. We are strong when we are weak (2 Cor. 12:9, 10), for God is strangely near to the broken-hearted (Psa. 34:18). In Genesis 28 Jacob bargained with God; in Genesis 32 he rested on him.

It is a sad truth that we usually delve far more deeply into the truths of the Christian faith in times

[5] See John MacArthur, *Safe in the Arms of God* (Nashville, TN: Thomas Nelson Publishers, 2003), p. 87.

of turmoil and suffering than in times of bliss and prosperity. It is chastening and affliction that teach us the need for obedience and which yield the peaceable fruit of righteousness (Psa. 119:67, 71, 75; Heb 12:4-11). The Welsh hymn-writer and evangelist, William Williams (Pantycelyn), declared that he acquired more knowledge of himself and the goodness of God while on his deathbed than he had during the previous forty years of his life.[6] In the words of the Puritan Richard Baxter: 'suffering so unbolts the door of the heart, that the word hath easier entrance.'[7] We suddenly find we have ears to hear, and God's word speaks to us, perhaps more directly and with greater unction than it ever had before.

God uses suffering to make the believer more compassionate and better able to minister to others. A friend of Amy Carmichael once said: 'A woman who has no experiences in the dark has no secrets to share in the light.'[8] To the wayward congregation at Corinth, the apostle Paul wrote:

[6] Cited in E. Houghton *Christian Hymn-writers* (Bridgend: Evangelical Press of Wales, 1982), p. 116.

[7] Richard Baxter, *The Saints' Everlasting Rest* (Grand Rapids, MI: Baker, 1978), p. 246.

[8] Cited in Sharon W. Betters, *Treasures in Darkness: A Grieving Mother Shares Her Heart*, (Phillipsburg, NJ: P&R, 2005), p. 13.

> Blessed be the God and Father of our Lord Jesus Christ, the Father of mercies and God of all comfort, who comforts us in all our tribulation, that we may be able to comfort those who are in any trouble, with the comfort with which we ourselves are comforted by God. For as the sufferings of Christ abound in us, so our consolation also abounds through Christ (2 Cor. 1:3-5).

This biblical truth is movingly illustrated in the life of Robert Lewis Dabney. In 1855 the Southern Presbyterian theologian lost two sons, and in 1862 was to endure the death of a third. About the year 1859 he visited the home of a couple whose only child, a little boy, lay ill with fever. A pastor's wife, who was present, recalled of Dabney:

> Soon he walked to the bed, and kneeling near the mother, gave way to a flood of tears such as I then thought I had never seen a man weep. Then he offered such a prayer as you can well imagine that great tender heart, so recently bereaved, would offer for the afflicted parents, and the precious child then almost in the Saviour's arms.[9]

If love is, in the poet James McAuley's words, 'how to mean the other's being,' there can be no doubt that Dabney's own suffering enabled him later to

[9] T. C. Johnson, *The Life and Letters of Robert Lewis Dabney* (Edinburgh: Banner of Truth Trust, 1977), p. 178.

minister to others with such deep compassion. One grieving mother remembered those who visited her in her sadness, but added: 'One that particularly stands out in my mind was from a man who didn't say much, but simply sat with me and cried.'[10]

We are wired to look for quick solutions. If the water pipe has burst, I am keen to find a plumber to fix it; if my back aches, I want the doctor to alleviate the pain as soon as possible. Grief, however, is different. I want a solution or some comfort, yes, but an instant one only makes matters worse. For suffering parents or grandparents or siblings, the first need is not someone who wants to cheer us up. That can come further down the track. The immediate need – and perhaps the need for quite a while – is the reassurance that deep lament is met with deep empathy.

As our little Emily was passing from this life, the journey was not one which immediately expanded my sympathy for others. There were hints of that, but overall my world felt like it was shrinking, to one precious little five year old girl who was fading before our eyes. It seemed like I thought of her all day, every day, and not much else mattered. John

[10] Cited in Glenda Mathes, *Little One Lost: Living with Early Infant Loss* (Grandville, MI: Reformed Fellowship, Inc, 2012), p. 129.

Chrysostom pointed out that we centre on our sorrows:

> As they who suffer pain in any part of their bodies, think that their sufferings exceed their neighbour's. He that has a disease of the eye thinks there is nothing so painful, and he that has a disorder of the stomach, considers that the sorest of diseases, and each thinks that the heaviest of suffering, with which he is himself afflicted. So it is with sorrow, each thinks his own present grief the most severe.[11]

Or, to quote the poet Emily Dickinson:

> I measure every Grief I meet
> With narrow, probing, Eyes –
> I wonder if It weighs like Mine –
> Or has an Easier size.[12]

That, sad to say, was my immediate experience. 'Old age came suddenly by suffering sped,' wrote Boethius.[13] Outwardly, as a Christian pastor, I tried to empathise with the sufferings of others, all the while thinking that theirs could not possibly be

[11] John Chrysostom, *Homilies on Timothy*, Oxford edition with additions by Philip Schaff, in *Nicene and Post-Nicene Fathers*, vol. XIII (Grand Rapids, MI: Eerdmans, 1979), on 2 Timothy 1:7, p. 478.

[12] Emily Dickinson, *The Complete Poems*, edited by Thomas H. Johnson (London: Faber and Faber, 2016), no. 561, p. 272.

[13] Boethius, *Consolation of Philosophy*, Book 1, p. 35.

compared to mine, or to that of my granddaughter and her family. Sharing the joy of the safe arrival of other children became tinged with an ungodly envy, and inability to enter fully into the happiness of others. The apostle Paul looked outward, but I was being pressed inward. It has been an ongoing battle to recapture a greater sense of empathy for others.

For all this, the main blessing that comes to the Christian through his suffering is that it drives him to focus his attention more closely upon the city which is to come. The Christian realises that his suffering is but for a short time (John 16:21; 2 Cor. 4:17), and cannot be compared to the glory which is to come (Rom. 8:18). One of our major problems in this life is that we tend to focus only on this world, and so we need to be weaned from the wrong sort of attachment to it. From 1858 to 1862 Rev. John William Matheson and his wife Mary laboured to bring the gospel of salvation to Tanna in the New Hebrides, or what is now called Vanuatu. They battled on, enduring very poor health and the loss of their infant daughter. Yet they retained their Christian perspective, and Mary Matheson affirmed: 'One moment in heaven will amply compensate for all we have suffered here.'[14] All Christians must seek to cultivate that same outlook.

There are dangers all around. Of itself, time does not heal, not immediately, nor even further down life's journey. In fact, the second year of sorrow may be a greater burden to bear than the first year. Faith is not a quick fix. Nor is it to be confused with a death wish which is dressed up in the language of a yearning for escaping this prison and embracing eternal life. About the year AD 115, Ignatius of Antioch was led to Rome to be martyred for his faith in Christ. His letters contain some startling lines:

> May nothing seen or unseen fascinate me, so that I may happily make my way to Jesus Christ! Fire, cross, struggles with wild beasts, wrenching of bones, mangling of limbs, crunching of the whole body, cruel tortures inflicted by the devil – let them come upon me, provided only I make my way to Jesus Christ ... Forgive me, brethren; do not obstruct my coming to life – do not wish me to die; do not make a gift to the world of one who wants to be God's. Beware of seducing me with matter; suffer me to receive pure light. Once arrived there, I shall be a man (*Rom.* 5, 3-6).

[14] G. Patterson *Memoirs of the Rev. S. F Johnston, the Rev. J. W. Matheson, and Mrs Mary Matheson* (Philadelphia: W. S. & A. Martien, 1864), p. 451.

In another letter he wrote:

> Why, moreover, did I surrender myself to death, to fire, to the sword, to wild beasts? Well, to be near the sword is to be near God; to be in the claws of wild beasts is to be in the hands of God. Only let it be done in the name of Jesus Christ! To suffer with him I endure all things, if he, who became perfect man, gives me the strength (*Smyrn.* 4, 2).[15]

In 1840 Alexander Carson commented regarding Ignatius: 'His letters are rather a sort of pious raving about the glories of martyrdom.'[16] It is hard to disagree. There is something unhealthy and escapist about such sentiments, for all Ignatius' bravery. Christians appreciate life as God's good gift, and it is costly to give it up.

The *Shorter Catechism* famously declares that man's chief end is to glorify God and to enjoy him forever. This points us to the resurrection of the dead. The time has not yet come when Christ will raise the dead by his word. But when he judges all humanity, some will be raised to a resurrection of life, some to a resurrection of judgment (John 5:28,

[15] See William Schoedel, *Ignatius of Antioch* (Philadelphia, PA: Fortress, 1985).

[16] Alexander Carson, *The History of Providence as Manifested in Scripture* (1840; repr. Edinburgh: Banner of Truth Trust, 2012), p. 189.

29). However, God has given us previews of that great day. The firstfruits of the harvest of believers is the resurrection of the Lord Jesus Christ (1 Cor. 15:20, 23).

God has given us other proofs too. On a number of occasions in Scripture God reveals his power by raising the dead. It is significant that many of these occasions concerned children. In the Gospels we read of numerous raisings from the dead, but we have more detailed records of only three – Lazarus (John 11), the widow of Nain's son (Luke 7:11-17), and Jairus' daughter (Luke 8:40-56). Of these three, two were children. In the Old Testament we also find that God raised children from the dead, notably the son of the widow at Zarephath during Elijah's ministry (1 Kings 17:17-24), and the son of the Shunammite woman during Elisha's ministry (2 Kings 4:18-37).

Nor are these the only indications that we have of God's special concern for children. One of the terrible sufferings that Job endured was the loss of his ten beloved children, for whom he had prayed and offered sacrifices daily (Job 1:1-5, 18, 19). In the midst of his anguish, Job maintained his faith in his living Redeemer who at the last would raise his people from the dead (Job 19:25-27). Later, when God greatly blessed Job, he promised him double of all that he had lost beforehand (Job 42:10-12;

cf. 1:3). However, Job did not receive back twenty children, but only another ten (Job 42:13). The point is that he had not lost the first ten; they had only been removed from him for a time.

God's covenant love goes to his people and to their descendants (Gen. 17:10; Deut. 29:10-14). The gospel promises in the New Testament are for 'you and for your children' (Acts 2:39). Even a pagan Gentile heard the message: 'Believe in the Lord Jesus, and you will be saved, you and your household' (Acts 16:31). The covenant and its sign, baptism, do not automatically save anyone, but children of the covenant are said to be 'holy,' set apart in some way by God (1 Cor. 7:14). As Flavel says: 'Scripture speaks very favourably of them.'[17]

For the Christian, there is hope underlying his grief. 'All now mysterious shall be bright at last,' wrote Katharina von Schlegel, and it will prove to be so. Hence the soliloquy:

> Be still, my soul: thy Jesus can repay,
> From His own fullness, all He takes away.

It is the Messiah, the suffering servant, who heals the brokenhearted (Psa. 34:18; 147:3; Isa. 61:1). 'Those who sow in tears shall reap with shouts of joy!' (Psa. 126:5) 'For we do not have a high priest

[17] John Flavel, *Facing Grief*, p. 108.

who is unable to sympathise with our weaknesses, but one who in every respect has been tempted as we are, yet without sin. Let us then with confidence draw near to the throne of grace, that we may receive mercy and grace to help in time of need' (Heb. 4:15, 16).

The renowned eighteenth-century hymn-writer and Methodist preacher, Charles Wesley, lost five of his eight children. He expressed his grief in poetry, the language of the heart:

> Faith cries out, It is the Lord!
> Let Him do as seems Him good.
> Be Thy holy name adored,
> Take the gift awhile bestowed;
> Take the child no longer mine,
> Thine he is, forever Thine.[18]

Unbelief cries; faith cries out – the difference is life-giving.

We find this hope sustaining the saints throughout all human history. In September 1542 Magdalene, a thirteen-year-old daughter of the great German Reformer, Martin Luther, lay dying of the plague. Her father asked her: 'Magdalene, my dear little daughter, would you like to stay here with your father, or would you willingly go to your

[18] Cited in James W. Bruce III, *From Grief to Glory* (Edinburgh: Banner of Truth Trust, 2008), p. 31.

Father yonder?' Magdalene replied: 'Darling father, as God wills.' Luther prayed and wept that God might free her, and before long Magdalene died in his arms. As his daughter was laid in her coffin, Luther declared:

> Darling Lena, you will rise and shine like a star, yea, like the sun ... I am happy in spirit, but the flesh is sorrowful and will not be content, the parting grieves me beyond measure ... I have sent a saint to heaven.[19]

It is the assurance of resurrection that contained Luther's grief and made it bearable.

The same faith sustained Andrew Bonar in his trials. In 1860 his little son, also called Andrew, died. The grieving father looked ahead to the resurrection day: 'O to see him come with Christ, to recognise that sweet, sweet voice amid the company of the redeemed!'[20] Four years later Bonar's wife Isabella died, and Bonar wrote in his diary: 'I have been thinking of her in glory, perhaps with little Andrew beside her, and how they will meet me!'[21]

[19] Cited in E. G. Rupp and B. Drewery (eds), *Martin Luther* (London: Edward Arnold, 1971), p. 162.

[20] Andrew A. Bonar, *Diary and Life* (Edinburgh: Banner of Truth Trust, 1984), p. 201.

[21] Ibid., p. 227.

Can we have a well-grounded hope that children who die will dwell with God forever? Some have hesitated to say more than that the only comfort given by God is to *Christians*. John Owen, for example, did not believe that dying infants of Muslims, pagans or infidels were saved. So pronounced were his views on original sin that he considered such a notion 'absolutely destructive to the free grace of God.'[22] The reader may struggle here, especially if weighed down by sorrow, but God did order the complete destruction of the tribes which we conveniently label together as the Canaanites. They were devoted to complete destruction, what was called the 'ban' (the *herem*; Deut. 7:1-5; see Josh. 6:21 for the taking of Jericho). Something similar is at work with the death of all the firstborn – of man and beast – in Egypt as God prepared to release his captive people (Exod. 12:29, 30).

To return to the Canaanites, no mercy was to be shown; it was to be a time of almost unrelieved justice (the exception being the saving of Rahab and her household). Much outrage has been expressed at this view of God. Yet it points us to the judgment of God at the end of history. The entry

[22] John Owen, *Works*, vol. X (Edinburgh: Banner of Truth Trust, 1976), p. 399.

of Israel into the Promised Land was to coincide with the forced eviction of the Canaanites from it. God was slow to express his wrath, and waited for over four hundred years, from giving the promise to Abraham to acting on it. Only when the iniquity of the Amorites was complete did God judge the Canaanites (Gen. 15:16). Moreover, one of the many reasons for God's condemnation of the Canaanites was their abominable practice of child sacrifice (Lev. 18:21).

A child might be taken for God's good reasons which are unknown to us. Whatever the case, we are at the edge of what God has clearly revealed to us. The Judge of all the earth does justly (Gen. 18:25). He is slow to anger and abounding in steadfast love and faithfulness (Exod. 34:6). Our hope is to be anchored in the character of God.

We must face the truth that we are all born as children of wrath, dead in trespasses and sins (Eph. 2:1-3). So for the salvation of children, we look not to the supposed sinlessness of children – it is not there – but the free and electing loving kindness of God's grace. On this ground, John Newton hesitated to speculate too much, but was hopeful for the salvation of all infants who died,[23] while

[23] *The Works of John Newton*, ed. by Richard Cecil, vol. 6 (1820; repr. Edinburgh: Banner of Truth Trust, 1985), pp.

Charles Spurgeon spoke even more decidedly, as he contemplated the multitudes of the redeemed: 'I rejoice to know that the souls of all infants, as soon as they die, speed their way to paradise.'[24]

The apostolic word of John offers yet greater comfort. He was granted visions of heaven, God's dwelling place, and finally of the new heaven and new earth. Utopias on earth turn out to be nightmares, but John saw what cannot be thwarted by human limitations and sin:

> After this I looked, and behold, a great multitude that no one could number, from every nation, from all tribes and peoples and languages, standing before the throne and before the Lamb, clothed in white robes, with palm branches in their hands, and crying out with a loud voice, 'Salvation belongs to our God who sits on the throne and to the Lamb!' (Rev. 7:9, 10).

Amongst the great number of the redeemed – who are in fact as numerous as the stars of heaven and the sand on the seashore (Gen. 22:17) – there

---

182-83. [2015 ed., vol. 4, p. 419]

[24] See C. H. Spurgeon, *No Tears in Heaven* (Fearn, Ross-shire: Christian Focus, 2021, pp. 70-71). See too Neil Cullan McKinlay, *Are All Who Die in Infancy Saved? (*WEEMAC Publishing, 2020); B. B. Warfield, *The Development of the Doctrine of Infant Salvation* (New York: The Christian Literature Co, 1891); and John MacArthur, *Safe in the Arms of God.*

will be millions upon millions of those who were children when they left this earth.

The new heaven and new earth has ever been the Christian hope, never so beautifully expressed as by Augustine as he contemplated the beatific vision: 'He will be the goal of all our longings; and we shall see him for ever; we shall love him without satiety; we shall praise him without wearying. This will be the duty, the delight, the activity of all, shared by all who share the life of eternity.'[25] 'For,' he asked, 'what is our end but to reach that kingdom which has no end?'[26]

[25] Augustine, *City of God*, trans. by H. Bettenson (Harmondsworth: Penguin, 1972), XXII, 30.

[26] Ibid.

3

Helping Those Who Grieve

We know so little, and the worst response is to pretend that we know more than we do. Patience is much needed – by others towards those who are grieving, and by the grieving towards themselves. We all like to solve sad situations quickly, but this can do more harm than good.

Perhaps the reader has known the agony of losing a child, a grandchild, a sibling, or perhaps even children. Anniversaries are times of reflection and pain; that which is meant to delight fails to deliver. You feel love but the recipient of that love is gone from this world. Emily Dickinson captured something of the sense:

> The Bustle in a House
> The Morning after Death
> Is solemnest of industries
> Enacted upon Earth –

> The Sweeping up the Heart
> And putting Love away
> We shall not want to use again
> Until Eternity.[1]

Something like this is at work, but it is not that love disappears. Rather, it cannot be acted upon in the same way.

You have asked yourself: 'What will the future be like without my child? How can I go on?' Or even, 'How can I ever give myself to another child again, as I may lose him or her too, and go through this pain again?' If children are a gift from the Lord (Psa. 127:3), how could he take back that precious gift? Life can seem pointless and empty. Often people do not know what to say, and some manage to say the wrong thing. Singing songs to a heavy heart only makes matters worse (Prov. 25:20). Those who try to help may actually frustrate and even hurt, albeit unwittingly. We have probably all heard someone offer the banal and unworthy suggestion that God needed the deceased child in heaven. The God of the Bible does not need anything (Acts 17:25).

It is not uncommon to hear the advice that one should put aside all sadness and move on with life. C. S. Lewis almost became irritable at some attempts to alleviate his situation when his wife died: 'It is hard

[1] Dickinson, *Complete Poems*, No. 1078, p. 489.

to have patience with people who say "There is no death" or "Death doesn't matter." There is death. And whatever is matters … You might as well say that birth doesn't matter.'[2] Joy matters, sorrow matters, truth matters, sin matters. Nothing is trivial, least of all the issues of God and eternity.

John Calvin is often said to be almost a Stoic in his approach to life. Do not believe it. You who grieve, take comfort from Calvin's response to the death from plague of a young man named Louis. Louis was a promising son of a Monsieur de Richebourg, and he had treated Calvin as 'another father.' On hearing of Louis' death in 1541, Calvin wrote to the sorrowing father:

> When I first received the intelligence of the death of … your son Louis, I was so utterly overpowered that for many days I was fit for nothing but to grieve; and albeit I was somehow upheld before the Lord by those aids wherewith he sustains our souls in affliction, among men, however, I was almost a nonentity; so far at least as regards my discharge of duty, I appeared to myself quite as unfit for it as if I had been half dead.[3]

[2] C. S. Lewis, *A Grief Observed* (London: Faber and Faber, 1966), p. 15.

[3] John Calvin, *Tracts and Letters*, vol. 4, edited by Jules Bonnet, trans. by David Constable (Edinburgh: Banner of Truth Trust, 2009), p. 246.

A year later, Calvin was to experience such sadness in his own household. In August 1542 he wrote to Pierre Viret: 'The Lord has certainly inflicted a severe and bitter wound in the death of our infant son. But he is himself a Father, and knows best what is good for his children.'[4] In his relatively brief marriage to Idelette van Buren, from 1540 to 1549, all three of their infant children died. The saints are not preserved from sadness.

Then there are those who say or imply that having another child will replace the one who has died. Another child is good, but no child can replace the one who has departed. Others may offer advice like 'Think positive and don't dwell on your loss. You can get over it.' Others simply fumble. When Boswell's son, David, died, Dr Johnson wrote: 'You must remember, that to keep three out of four is more than your share. Mrs Thrale has but four out of eleven.'[5] Even John Newton, whose insights into the pastoral care of the human soul are gems of wisdom and grace, could be rather clumsy here. He once wrote to one grieving couple: 'I hope you are both well reconciled to the death of your child. Indeed, I cannot be sorry for the death

[4] Ibid., p. 344.

[5] James Boswell, *The Life of Samuel Johnson* (London: Dent, 1973), vol. 2, p. 79.

of infants. How many storms do they escape!'[6] It is not that this is not true – it is – but it could use a little less bluntness and a touch more tenderness of expression.

Well-meaning sympathisers may say: 'Call me if you need anything,' but the grieving parent or grandparent is usually not aware of what is needed, nor in a fit condition to ask for it. Friends of sorrowing parents ought not to learn too much from Job's three friends, yet there are insights to be gleaned from their attempt to comfort Job after he lost his livelihood, his ten precious children, and his health (see Job 1–2). These three friends are often roundly criticised, but they start better than they finish. Nancy Guthrie's *What Grieving People Wish You Knew*, written in the aftermath of the deaths from Zellweger syndrome of two of her children, Hope and Gabriel, is enormously realistic and incisive. It will help us as we look at Job's three friends who came to comfort him. One receives the impression that they turned up fairly soon after Job's tragedies, but the gap may have been some time, even months (see Job 7:3).

Looking ahead in the book of Job, we know what happens. The three friends meet Job in Job

[6] *The Works of John Newton*, vol. 6 (1820; repr. Edinburgh: Banner of Truth Trust, 1985), p. 182. (2015 ed., vol. 4, p. 419).

2:11-13, but in the next chapter Job loses it, and curses the day of his birth (Job 3). The three friends are drawn into what appears to be an unproductive slanging match where they say that Job is suffering greatly because he has sinned greatly. As Job pushes back, he becomes more incorrigible, and his three friends become more censorious and severe. It is easy to misinterpret all this. The three friends are good and believing men. At the end we find not that Job is one hundred percent right and his three friends one hundred percent wrong, but that Job is more right than wrong, and his three friends more wrong than right. Life can be like that.

Job's comforters are not model comforters, but they do deserve a fair and sympathetic reading. In Job 2:11-13 we are told:

> Now when Job's three friends heard of all this evil that had come upon him, they came each from his own place, Eliphaz the Temanite, Bildad the Shuhite, and Zophar the Naamathite. They made an appointment together to come to show him sympathy and comfort him. And when they saw him from a distance, they did not recognise him. And they raised their voices and wept, and they tore their robes and sprinkled dust on their heads toward heaven. And they sat with him on the ground seven days and seven nights, and no

> one spoke a word to him, for they saw that his suffering was very great.

What began as a pastoral visit turned into a verbal wrestling match – but not yet!

(a) Make contact.

Sometimes we are hesitant to make contact when someone has suffered great grief. We are not sure what to do, so we don't do anything. We are not obliged to intrude into everybody's life, but these friends are friends. They travel considerable distances to reach Job, when others had deserted him. Job laments later: 'My relatives have failed me, my close friends have forgotten me' (Job 19:14). These are not among the thousands of Facebook friends that one may accumulate simply because it makes us feel influential and popular. Surely they are to be commended as true friends: 'A man of many companions may come to ruin, but there is a friend who sticks closer than a brother' (Prov. 18:24).

As you suffer the loss of your child, it will surprise you who makes contact and who does not. Resentment against those who fail to contact you in any meaningful way is a temptation that must be resisted. Grief fuels fear (what if God does this again?) and loneliness (people can be kind but they do not really share in this isolation), but beware of a bitter spirit which demands some kind of retribution (this has to be someone's fault). We easily become jaundiced; and our judgments skewed. Over time, too, the sufferer needs to recall that others will move on when you have not, and cannot. You never will, not entirely, in this life.

Drawing on Isaiah 53:3, 4, Joseph Scriven penned lines that have comforted many a sorrowing saint:

> What a Friend we have in Jesus!
> All our sins and griefs to bear.

The Saviour bears our sins. He endured our hell that we might enjoy his heaven. Yet he also bears our griefs. We cannot do for ourselves or for others what only Jesus can do, and we cannot demand more from people than what they can deliver.

Do not turn analysis into paralysis. Christ-centred comfort is the best we can offer. This begins with making contact. Job's three friends started off by doing what they could.

(b) Aim to offer sympathy and comfort.

From Job 4–31 there are twenty-eight chapters where the friendship descends into a painful debate about God and suffering, and whether Job deserved what he got. When the Bible was better known, the expression 'Job's comforters' was used to describe those who failed to offer comfort but instead made matters worse by accusing. The point here is that they did not start out that way; they intended to do what friends do. Where they start from and where they end up are two different places. 'The beginning of strife is like letting out water, so quit before the quarrel breaks out' (Prov. 17:14). It must be understood that the three friends did not intend initially to cause strife.

(c) Show sympathy and comfort.

Job was so affected by his suffering that his countenance had changed so much that they did not recognise him (2:12). I remember experiencing this with a woman at Nambucca who suffered for about four years with a debilitating but unknown disease before she died. She was a regular attender at church, then went to hospital, then to a nursing home. In the space of a few days she changed, so much so that when I was looking for her in the nursing home I did not recognise her at first. Job's three friends were looking for him, but did not recognise him immediately. That is what suffering can do to one.

The three friends tore their robes and sprinkled dust on their heads – all very middle eastern. They are not having coffee together; they are sitting with him in the rubbish dump. They wept with one who wept, as we are all bidden to do (Rom. 12:15). Calvin is right: 'They do not come to mock Job. They bring with them no malice or ill will, but they have a complete and sincere love for him.'[7] They genuinely felt his affliction.

(d) Sometimes silence is better than words.

They sat in silence before Job for a week (2:13). Here is what Nancy Guthrie says: 'A person who is sad doesn't necessarily need to be cheered up but needs time, space, and permission to simply be sad for a while.' She gives some good advice: 'Do not say anything that starts with "Well, at least ..." That adds to the pain. "Do not say that God needed the person in heaven." That is just sentimentality. "Do not say that you know someone else who ..." That can come later. Do not ask, "How are you?" The answer is "I am miserable."'[8]

Mrs Guthrie advises, rightly, that the name of the deceased person is music to the ears of one who is grieving. It takes the person seriously. And

[7] John Calvin, *Sermons on Job, Chapters 1–14*, trans. by Rob Roy McGregor, vol. 1 (Edinburgh: Banner of Truth Trust, 2022), p. 114.

[8] See Guthrie, *What Grieving People Wish You Knew*, pp. 38-68.

it is quite in order to say: 'I do not know what to say.' No words can be adequate. Do not feel the pressure to come up with something wonderfully wise and consoling. If you are struggling to be helpful, say so.[9]

Seven days was the period of mourning in extreme situations (Lam. 2:10; Ezek. 3:15). The friends may be implying that Job was as good as dead, or it may be for his ten children. Christopher Ash sees this as silence before the dead, and David Atkinson calls it 'the compassion of a silent presence.' So far, so good. Later a sarcastic Job thinks they would have been better off just being there and saying nothing: 'Oh that you would keep silent, and it would be your wisdom!' (13:5).

At the first stage of terrible tragedy, it is better just to show empathy and not try to say too much. Words can seem glib at such a time. Helmut Thielicke, who lived through the period of the Confessing Church's resistance to Hitler in Germany, once said that the greatest defect in American Christians was their inadequate view of suffering.[10] It is no doubt true of all Christians, and not always for totally bad reasons. The new

[9] Ibid., pp. 58-59.

[10] Cited in Philip Yancey, *Where is God When it Hurts?* (Grand Rapids, MI: Zondervan, 1977), p. 15.

heaven and the new earth, after all, will be a place where suffering has been forever abolished. In the Garden of Eden we were wired to live without sin and suffering and death. The vestiges of that remains. Otherwise, joy would not be so appealing, and suffering so appalling.

We are impatient people, more impatient than Job's three friends. But we cannot short-circuit suffering. If we are in Christ, the boat will regain some kind of equilibrium in time. Shortcuts are no answer. So far Job's three friends have done all what was humanly possible. Here is costly care; here is sympathy and comfort; and here is a sensitive empathy. Nancy Guthrie comments: 'To be a patient friend over the long haul of grief requires a lot of dying to self and serving another.'[11]

[11] Guthrie, *What Grieving People Wish You Knew*, p. 109.

4
God's Final Word

Perhaps we can now try to summarise some of the biblical comfort and challenge that the death of a child brings to Christians.

First, the Christian must not be ashamed to feel grief and sorrow.

The Christian is not a Stoic who bravely stifles his emotions. 'Weep with those who weep,' writes the apostle Paul (Rom. 12:15). When Paul's fellow worker, Epaphroditus, almost died, the great apostle declared that he would have had sorrow upon sorrow had his friend actually departed this life (Phil. 2:27). Paul knew the power of the resurrection (Eph. 1:19, 20) and looked forward to his own death (Phil. 1:23), but this did not eradicate his capacity to experience anguish. To despair is sinful, but to grieve is not. When Charles Spurgeon lost a young grandson, he wrote in his own honest and heartfelt way to his grieving son and daughter-in-law: 'The Lord himself comfort you. I want comforting myself.'[1]

When we flee from affliction, either in ourselves or in others, we actually add to the pain. This life is real, sin is real, the curse is real, and death is real. Better to face it than flee from it. Sharon Betters lost her teenage son, Mark, in a car accident in July 1993. In her grief, she has advocated 'the treasure of journalling' in order to navigate this broken world, although she admits it has a frightening side.[2] The sovereignty of God will ultimately bring great comfort but at first it may increase the agony – God could have stopped the death but did not for reasons of his own. At first the Christian may be able to do no more than weep. Mrs Betters records: 'In the days after Mark's death, God did not robe me in a cocoon of peace and grace. Instead I suffocated in a garb of ghastly grief that I feared would strangle every breath of life out of me.'[3] She even speaks of being 'raped by death.'[4]

[1] Cited in James W. Bruce III, *From Grief to Glory*, p. 56.

[2] Betters, *Treasures in Darkness*, pp. 48, 51. See too Chapman and Vaughn, *Choosing to SEE*, pp. 207ff.

[3] Betters, *Treasures in Darkness*, p. 88.

[4] Ibid., p. 206.

These expressions of terrible grief are proof of the fallenness of the world, but are not in themselves sinful – not at all. Indeed, quite the reverse, according to Alec Motyer who comments: 'Tears are proper for believers – indeed they should be all the more copious, for Christians are more sensitively aware of every emotion, whether of joy or sorrow, than those who have known nothing of the softening and enlivening grace of God.'[5]

Secondly, reality must be faced.

As C. S. Lewis put it: 'There is nothing we can do with suffering except to suffer it.'[6] More needs to be said on this, but there is no comfort to be found in a flight from reality. When King David's child died after a week's illness, David ceased his fasting and weeping. This surprised his servants, but David asked: 'Can I bring him back again? I shall go to him, but he shall not return to me' (2 Sam. 12:23). Some grieving parents make-believe that the child is still with them, or else that the child never existed. David's attitude is much healthier – he recognised that life had to go on without his child. When Sir John Hartopp's infant

[5] J. A. Motyer, *The Message of Philippians* (Leicester: IVP, 1984), p. 90.

[6] Cited in Chapman and Vaughn, *Choosing to SEE*, p. 261.

daughter died, John Owen pointed the Hartopp family to the example of David: 'Your dear infant is in the eternal enjoyment of the fruits of all our prayers; for the covenant of God is ordered in all things, and sure. We shall go to her; she shall not return to us.'[7]

The Koop family too, after the tragedy of losing their son in 1968, came to this realisation: 'Of course, our family life never will be the same, but we are trusting in the Lord to help us accept the empty place in our family circle and to keep us constantly aware that David is in heaven – which is far better for him.'[8] The unbeliever has the same pain, but no real and lasting comfort. On 20 March 1991 Conor, the four-year-old son of the singer/guitarist Eric Clapton, exuberantly ran towards a window on the 53rd floor of the New York City apartment where his mother was staying, not realising that the window had been removed. The result was horrific beyond description. Clapton, whose life was riddled with infidelities and alcohol abuse, wrote of the 'terrible numbness' which encompassed him, and asked: 'Will we really meet

[7] *John Owen, Daily Readings*, ed. by Lee Gatiss (Fearn, Ross-shire: Christian Heritage, 2022), introducing November.

[8] C. Everett and Elizabeth Koop, *Sometimes Mountains Move*, p. 44.

again?'[9] In a haunting song co-written with Will Jennings, he imagined himself visiting heaven and meeting Conor there:

> Would you know my name
> If I saw you in heaven?
> Would it be the same
> If I saw you in heaven?

The pain is devastating as Clapton concludes:

> I must be strong
> And carry on,
> 'Cause I know I don't belong
> Here in heaven.

Clapton wrote of God, the twelve-step recovery programme, and salvation through music. Too much is missing and distorted. Only the gospel of Christ crucified, risen, and triumphant can preserve us from such unending and hopeless tragedy. Without the Light of the world, the darkness is dark indeed.

The Christian position is not the fanciful one that children are in heaven because they are obviously sinless. As we have noted, the Bible makes it clear that as children we all inherit sin and death (Psa. 51:5; Rom. 5:12-21; 1 Cor. 15:22;

[9] Eric Clapton, *Clapton: The Autobiography* (New York: Broadway Books, 2007), p. 250.

Eph. 2:3). Children do have an innocence about them (cf. Jon. 4:11; Jer. 19:4-7), but the Christian position is that children are saved first because of God's electing grace. When Israel rebelled in the wilderness and so a whole generation was excluded from the Promised Land, the children were exempt from this judgment (Deut. 1:39). The Saviour himself welcomed children and said: 'Let them come to me; do not hinder them, for to such belongs the kingdom of God' (Mark 10:14). The Son of God has a special love for children.

At the risk of wounding when the task ought to be healing, one should point out that children do not remain children in the new heaven and new earth. Oliver Gill was born on 10 July 2010, to a Christian couple, Andy and Jennifer. However, Oliver came into this world with a rare and aggressive form of cancer, which claimed his short life on Christmas Day of the same year. One understands – because their only experience of Oliver was as a little baby – but still winces a little when the Gills write of cuddling young Oliver in heaven, and having him in their arms forever. Somehow they have to try to envisage Oliver as they knew him, and as he is in glory.[10] I have the

[10] Andy and Jennifer Gill, *Love Oliver* (Fearn, Ross-shire: Christian Focus, 2011), pp. 111, 126.

same difficulty with young Emily. She was only given five years on earth, so I cannot think of her as a teenager or an adult, a worker of some kind, a wife or a mother. She remains a young child in my thinking, and must remain so for this life. But that cannot be the final word.

Some of the mediaeval theologians speculated that the redeemed in the new heaven and new earth will resemble Adam and Eve when they were created – meaning, in earthly terms, they will look about thirty years of age. It is hard to envisage the new heaven and new earth being populated with children who are forever children, and aged people who are forever old, or disfigured people who forever look disfigured. Christ rose with his wounds still visible (see John 20:24-28), and even in the apostle John's vision of heaven, Christ appears as the Lion who rules and the Lamb 'standing as though it had been slain' (Rev. 5:6). That, surely, would reflect the uniqueness of Christ, and the eternal significance of his sufferings. Those who belong to Christ will not carry their physical, moral and spiritual shortcomings into the resurrection life.

There are various coping mechanisms. Some think that they will cope better if they try to forget the child; others are almost consumed by a fear that they might forget the child. There are some places that you might avoid because the memories are too deep and too traumatic. Cameron Cole records that he would drive five minutes out of his way to avoid the entrance of the children's hospital emergency department where his three-year-old son was pronounced dead.[11] Many feel an obligation to prolong their unhappiness out of respect for the deceased; others cast themselves into an unreal round of pleasure-seeking. But the Christian is neither to dwell on the past nor to ignore it. Rather, he is to remember it, and to press on, as Paul says, 'toward the goal for the prize of the upward call of God in Christ Jesus' (Phil 3:14).

Thirdly, the Lord calls us to commit ourselves to him. When Job lost his ten children and went through such terrible anguish that he questioned God's justice, God did not answer all his questions. Job never knew *why*, but he did know *who*. Instead of answering questions, God did far more – he revealed himself as the omnipotent Creator and Lord who holds all things in his hands (Job 38–42). Job learnt that he did not have all the answers himself, but he was to trust the God who did have all the answers:

[11] Cameron Cole, *Therefore I Have Hope* (Wheaton, IL; Crossway, 2018), p. 72.

> When we cannot see our way;
> Let us trust and still obey.

So wrote Thomas Kelly (1769–1855). God makes everything worthwhile, even suffering. It is therefore touching to read Andy and Jennifer Gill declare that 'we would do it all again.'[12]

The Psalmist's experience is recorded to help wounded and hurting saints: 'If I say, "My foot slips," your mercy, O Lord, holds me up. In the multitude of my anxieties within me, your comforts delight my soul' (Psa. 94:18, 19). Life can weigh us down and oppress us, but God has spoken to such situations. There is a plaque which reads: 'You never know that Jesus is all you need until Jesus is all you have.' John MacArthur tells of one father who sat with his baby daughter for the twenty-two hours of her life. His wife, recovering from a Caesarean operation, was more asleep than awake so he was left to suffer alone. Yet as he held his dying daughter in his arms, he experienced a calm that could only have come from God: 'During those minutes, as I sat in great sadness holding the lifeless body of my daughter, I had an overwhelming sense that God was holding *me*.'[13]

[12] Gill, *Love Oliver*, p. 113.

[13] See John MacArthur, *Safe in the Arms of God*, p. 130.

Jonathan and Jacqueline Gibson lost a daughter, Leila, at 39 weeks, virtually full-term. Their son, Ben, asked about the moon: why at times it looks like a banana, and at other times like only half of it is present. Dr Gibson – a professor in Old Testament, a pastor, a husband and a father – would point out that the moon is always round. It is just that sometimes we cannot see all of it.[14] I have never heard of a better illustration of God's ever-present goodness, no matter what the circumstances of life. Indeed, the moon is always round, and God is always good (Psa. 100:5).

Fourthly, the Christian needs to keep his eyes upon Christ as the risen king of the new heaven and new earth.

The goal of the Christian pilgrimage is not reunion with the loved one but the praise and service of God. Nevertheless, meeting saved loved ones will be one of the many blessings that flow from salvation. As David heard of the death of his infant son, he declared: 'I shall go to him' (2 Sam. 12:23). David was not simply saying that he was mortal. Rather, he recognised that he would die, but in that kingdom that shall know no end he would meet

[14] Jonathan Gibson, *The Moon is Always Round* (Greensboro, NC: New Growth Press, 2019).

the son whom he had scarcely known in this life. Even the son of his adultery with Bathsheba – the son who was taken from him – was in glory forever.

The kindest of strangers may ask the most awkward of questions: 'How many children do you have?' It is best in most contexts to include the one who is no longer with you. It is at the very least a testimony to the hope that we have within us (1 Pet. 3:15). In 1945 Charles Williams, whom C. S. Lewis called his 'dearest friend,' died after a short and unexpected illness. Lewis felt the loss deeply, but was not dejected. He wrote of Williams' death: 'It has made the next world much more real and palpable.'[15] We look forward to happy events, like holidays and weddings. They put a spring in our step before they happen. How much more so ought the expectation of Christ's final victory! J. C. Ryle wrote:

> When the Lord Jesus Christ comes the second time the dead saints shall all be raised and the living shall be changed. They shall no longer have a vile mortal body, full of weaknesses and infirmities. They shall have a body like that of their risen Lord, without the slightest liability to sickness and pain.[16]

[15] Roger Lancelyn Green and Walter Hooper, *C. S. Lewis: A Biography* (Glasgow: Collins, 1974), p. 224.

[16] J. C. Ryle, *Christmas Thoughts*, ed. by Andrew Atherstone

This is the earthiness of heaven – not the escape of a bird from a cage, but a complete transformation. Christ has promised: 'I make all things new' (Rev. 21:5). The result is a spiritual body (1 Cor. 15:44), with the emphasis on both parts of the description.

Samuel Rutherford lost all but one of the children born to his first wife, and all six of the children born to his second wife. His letters emphasise that children are not ours but God's. God lends them to us for a time. Hence he would say to grieving Christian parents: 'she is not lost to you who is found to Christ.'[17] Our children are given by God to us; they are not our own. Death is to be viewed in those terms: 'your lease of him is expired.'[18] The child is not gone away, but gone before, and 'your cup is sugared with mercy.'[19]

Death leads many an unbeliever to try to extract as much fun out of this world as is possible because the time is short. However, death signifies to the Christian the length of eternity. We are all heading to the judgment where God will declare his verdict on our lives, and that verdict is forever. We all

(Edinburgh: Banner of Truth Trust, 2022), p. 68.

[17] *Letters of Samuel Rutherford*, edited by Andrew A. Bonar (Edinburgh: Banner of Truth Trust, 1984), e.g. pp. 41, 607.

[18] Ibid., p. 607.

[19] Ibid., p. 565.

have eternity in our hearts (Eccles. 3:11), and death wakens us up from our sinful neglect of that truth. The enormity of sin makes us aware that we cannot save ourselves, and the horror of death reinforces that same sense of utter dependence.

We live in a world of spiritual and moral death, which is reinforced by the physical death we see around us and experience within us. Nobody has captured this better than Charles Wesley:

> Father of Jesus Christ, my Lord,
> My Saviour and my Head;
> I trust in Thee, Whose powerful word
> Hath raised Him from the dead.
>
> I hope, against all human hope,
> Self-desperate, I believe;
> Thy quickening word shall raise me up,
> Thou shalt Thy Spirit give.

Never has dirt appeared to me so dank and cold as the dirt that covered little Emily's little grave; and never has the resurrection appeared so vital. Here, more than in any other place, I know why Charles Wesley wrote 'self-desperate, I believe.' Life moved on slowly. Every day I thought of Emily – as did the rest of the family. She had faced death with frustrations but with remarkably little fear, and loved to hear from a book on the Twenty-third Psalm.

The rest of us faced life with an abiding dread, and needed to dwell more on the Twenty-third Psalm.

I believe in Christ, I believe in his death to pay the penalty for the sins of his people, in my best moments I hate my sin, I believe Christ rose from the dead and so defeated death forever, I believe in life everlasting in the new heaven and new earth. There is peace, and yet peace is not complacency. I know something of what C. S. Lewis meant:

> It is easy to say you believe a rope to be strong and sound as long as you are merely using it to cord a box. But suppose you had to hang by that rope over a precipice.[20]

The little grave looks like a precipice; the night sky looks like a vast chasm. How insignificant we are! Or seem to be. Self-desperation is part of believing in Christ.

At the very place where all hope seems to have gone, it reappears, often with renewed depth of meaning. Robert Lewis Dabney buried his son, Jimmy, in November 1855. He recorded:

> As I stand by the little grave, and think of the poor ruined clay within, that was a few days ago so beautiful, my heart bleeds. But as I ask, 'Where is the soul whose beams gave that clay all its

[20] Lewis, *A Grief Observed*, p. 21.

> beauty and preciousness?' I triumph. Has it not already begun, with an infant voice, the praises of my Saviour?[21]

Dabney had vowed to uphold the *Westminster Confession of Faith*, but the first question from the *Heidelberg Catechism* is wonderfully framed:

> Q. 1: What is your only comfort in life and death? A: That I, with body and soul, both in life and death, am not my own, but belong unto my faithful Saviour Jesus Christ; who with his precious blood has fully satisfied for all my sins, and delivered me from all the power of the devil; and so preserves me that without the will of my heavenly Father not a hair can fall from my head; yea, that all things must be subservient to my salvation, wherefore by his Holy Spirit he also assures me of eternal life, and makes me heartily willing and ready, henceforth, to live unto him.

God is love (1 John 4:8) and God is sovereign over evil (Isa. 45:7), and God has made himself known in his eternal Son, the crucified and risen Saviour, Christ Jesus.

The little body lies in the cold earth, and the thought of such an end to this life is dreadful to contemplate, but Christ is risen from the dead, never to die again. He shares his victory with

[21] Johnson *Life and Letters of Robert Lewis Dabney*, p. 169.

us. The rotting little body will not be God's last word – not at all. 'The paths of glory lead but to the grave,' wrote Thomas Gray in his 'Elegy Written in a Country Churchyard,' but it is also true that the grave leads to glory. At the age of twenty-seven, and facing her second divorce, Cathy Baker walked through her local cemetery. It had a decisive impact upon her. As she contemplated where all earthly life leads, God spoke to her, and she would recall: 'My life began in a graveyard.'[22] She came to look to the risen Christ; the contemplation of universal death led to the reception of everlasting life.

A lifetime without the beloved child looks like torture, but it is only momentary (2 Cor. 4:17). God is working his purposes out and the result will be joy for evermore (Psa. 16:11). We shall see Christ and be made like him (1 John 3:1-3).

> There you shall see His face,
> And never, never sin;
> There from the rivers of His grace,
> Drink endless pleasures in.
>
> – Isaac Watts

> And You'll gather us together
> In Your arms of endless grace,

[22] Cathy Baker, 'What does the Bible say about visiting graves?' Christianity.com, 22 June 2022.

As Your Bride forever
When we see Your face.
– Bob Kauflin

Just as Christ's suffering won the salvation of sinners, so suffering here prepares us for the eternal weight of glory. Glory will be 'heavier' than grief; the path of sorrow leads to where sorrow is unknown. God puts our tears in a bottle (Psa. 56:8) before he wipes them all away (Rev. 7:17).

The gospel turns this world on its head. Even the Old Testament, for all its shadows (Heb. 10:1), declares that the day of death is better than the day of birth (Eccles. 7:1). How could this be? In 1734 Jonathan Edwards preached on this text, and sought to answer that question. For those outside of Christ, the day of death is a day of the most terrible gloom, but for those who are in Christ, it is far different. 'Though you mourn for your loss, you should rejoice at their gain.'[23] When we enter this world, we enter a mixed state which is trapped in sin and misery and death, but for one upon whom Christ has set his saving love, the day of death is one of joy, light, perfection, holiness, and glory. He or she joins the company of angels and the spirits of

[23] Michael D. McMullen (ed), *The Blessing of God: Previously Unpublished Sermons of Jonathan Edwards* (Nashville, TN: Broadman and Holman Publishers, 2003), p. 159.

the righteous made perfect (cf. Heb. 12:22-24) who will sing the praises of God and the Lamb forever. We will all die (Psa. 49:10; 89:48), but there will be a place where 'sorrow and sighing shall flee away' (Isa. 35:10; see 32:17). No man can see God and live (Exod. 33:20), but in Christ the pure in heart shall see God and live (Matt. 5:8). 'Christ gives such a soul a joyful welcome to the place of his residence, and into his eternal presence, and into the arms of his dear love.'[24]

For the Christian – the sinner who has repented of sin and entrusted his whole life to Christ as King and Saviour – the sorrow of losing a child is tempered by the truth of Christ's resurrection victory. The unbeliever is at a complete loss, but the Christian declares with Paul: 'Our citizenship is in heaven, from which we also eagerly wait for the Saviour, the Lord Jesus Christ, who will transform our lowly body that it may be conformed to his glorious body, according to the working by which he is able even to subdue all things to himself (Phil. 3:20, 21). People often speak of the afterlife in terms of becoming like angels, but here Scripture says that the bodies of believers will not conform to those of angels, but to that of the risen Messiah.

[24] Ibid., p. 158.

This can take place because Christ's power and victory will know no limits. The 'all things' to which Paul refers will know no exceptions, not even suffering and death. That was Paul's hope. God grant that it be yours too. God wipes away every tear and takes away all pain, even death itself (Rev. 21:4). Your grief need not be forever: 'Weeping may tarry for the night, but joy comes with the morning' (Psa. 30:5). The last letter, undated, written by Amy Carmichael was one sprawling question to do with a precious child: 'If so dear to me, what to him?'[25] The deepest refuge is the love of God in Christ Jesus.

Somewhere Elisabeth Elliot quotes from an unknown author: 'Grief never ends … but it changes. It's a passage, not a place to stay. Grief is not a sign of weakness, nor a lack of faith … It is the price of love.' That is beautifully expressed, and an indication that Christ makes all things well. The cross shows us that the greatest good comes from the greatest evil, the most euphoric triumph comes from the most excruciating pain, blessedness forever in the new heaven and new earth comes from one who was forsaken on earth. Most mysteriously,

[25] Amy Carmichael, *Candles in the Dark* (Fort Washington, MD: CLC Publications, 2017), p. 124.

and experienced only gradually, there is, as John Chrysostom put it, 'grief ... the mother of joy.'[26]

One searches for something powerful and comforting to say as a fitting conclusion. Everything seems inadequate – we stammer, says Spurgeon[27] – but these words of John Chrysostom from his sermons on First Corinthians, delivered while he was bishop of Antioch may be of help to some grieving Christian parent: '... have you lost a child? You have not lost him (or her); say not so. This thing is sleep, not death; removal, not destruction; a journeying from the worse unto the better.'[28]

'There are no graves in glory,'[29] says Spurgeon. We are scarred for life but not for eternity. In glory, character will be purified and perfected; victory will be complete; God will delight in his people and his people will delight in God; and Christians will dwell where God's will is carried out without any opposition or compromise. The lambs of the

[26] John Chrysostom, *Homilies on Philippians*, in *Nicene and Post-Nicene Fathers*, vol. XIII, ed by Philip Schaff (Grand Rapids, MI: Eerdmans, 1979), p. 255.

[27] Spurgeon, *No Tears in Heaven*, p. 84.

[28] John Chrysostom, *Homilies on the Corinthians*, trans. by Talbot W. Chambers, in *Nicene and Post-Nicene Fathers*, vol. XII, (Grand Rapids, MI: Eerdmans, 1983), p. 254 (slightly altered).

[29] Spurgeon, *No Tears in Heaven*, p. 91.

Good Shepherd will see Christ as he is (1 John 3:2) – not as in a mirror darkly, not struggling in Gethsemane, nor abandoned on the cross, but reigning in the fullness of his perfect beauty and holiness and kindness.

As Job exclaimed: 'How my heart yearns within me' (Job 19:27).

It yearns indeed.

Dear Emily! Dear Saviour!

Amen.

BANNER of TRUTH

The Banner of Truth Trust originated in 1957 in London. The founders believed that much of the best literature of historic Christianity had been allowed to fall into oblivion and that, under God, its recovery could well lead not only to a strengthening of the church, but to true revival.

Interdenominational in vision, this publishing work is now international, and our lists include a number of contemporary authors, together with classics from the past. The translation of these books into many languages is encouraged.

A monthly magazine, *The Banner of Truth*, is also published, and further information about this, and all our other publications, may be found on our website, banneroftruth.org, or by contacting the offices below:

Head Office:
3 Murrayfield Road
Edinburgh
EH12 6EL
United Kingdom

Email: info@banneroftruth.co.uk

North America Office:
610 Alexander Spring Road
Carlisle, PA 17015
United States of America

Email: info@banneroftruth.org